EUROTUNNEL

Editorial:	Steve Parker
Design:	David West
	Children's Book Design
Illustrator:	Simon Bishop
Picture research:	Cecilia Weston-Baker

© Aladdin Books Ltd 1990

First published in
the United States in 1990 by
Gloucester Press
387 Park Avenue South
New York NY 10016

Printed in Belgium

Library of Congress Cataloging-in-Publication Data
Bender, Lionel.
    Eurotunnel / Lionel Bender.
        p.   cm. -- (Engineers at work)
    Summary: Examines one of the longest international construction
projects ever undertaken, the Channel Tunnel, the proposed tunnel linking
Europe and Great Britain.
    ISBN 0-531-17178-7
    1. Railroad tunnels--English Channel--Juvenile literature. [1. Railroad
tunnels--English Channel. 2. Tunnels.] I. Title. II. Series.
TF238.E5B46   1990
624.1'94'0916336--dc20   90-3238   CIP   AC

Contents

EUROTUNNEL

LIONEL BENDER

GLOUCESTER PRESS

London · New York · Toronto · Sydney

EUROTUNNEL

Even before the Battle of Hastings, in 1066, the histories of Britain and France were closely connected. But it was only in 1987 that the two countries signed a treaty to build a "fixed link" between them. Following this, the Anglo-French engineering company, Eurotunnel, was given a 55-year contract to build and operate a tunnel. It runs from near Folkestone in Kent, southeast England, to near Calais, in northeast France.

The "Eurotunnel" is bored through the seabed beneath the 21-mile-wide stretch of water between these two countries – the Channel, or la Manche. The Eurotunnel is also known as the Channel Tunnel, the Chunnel, and the TransManche Link. It is presenting engineers with a whole new world of challenges.

Eurotunnel consists, in fact, of three tunnels. The smaller central or service tunnel will provide ventilation and access for maintenance and emergency vehicles and people. High-speed intercity passenger trains, long-distance freight trains, and shuttle freight and tourist trains will all run through the main tunnels. Eurotunnel is due for completion in 1993.

▲ This, the first plan for a Channel tunnel, was put forward by French engineer Albert Mathieu-Favier in 1802. A French tunnel was started in 1877, and a British one in 1881 and again in 1975, but all three were abandoned.

Outgoing tunnel
This is 25 feet in diameter – about the size of a two-story house. Trains will run through it from London or from the terminal at Cheriton, near Folkestone.

The Eurotunnel
All three tunnels will be almost 31 miles in length, with 24 miles below the Channel. Eurotunnel will be the largest undersea transportation system in the world.

Locomotives
The 99 mph shuttle trains will be driven at both ends by electric locomotives powered from overhead cables.

Carriages and cars
Tourist shuttle trains will include 13 double-deck and 13 single-deck cars. The double-deckers will each take 120 automobiles and the single-deckers about 40 buses, or automobiles with trailers or campers.

Under the sea
Eurotunnel will be buried
between 56 and 131 feet
deep in the seabed.
Midway across the
Channel, it will be almost
328 feet below sea level.

Connecting panel

Service tunnel
This is 16 feet in diameter.
It contains a roadway and
is linked to the main
tunnels by cross-passages
every 1,230 feet.

Incoming tunnel
Identical in size to the
other main tunnel, this will
take trains from Paris and
from the shuttle terminal
at Coquelles near Calais.
Power lines, signaling and
communications cables
will be fixed to the walls.

THE PLANNING

The Eurotunnel Company had to draw up detailed engineering plans for approval by both governments. These had to show that their system was feasible and safe to use; how long and how much money it would take to build; how people, road and rail transportation would travel through it; and how the construction would not upset the environment more than was necessary. The result is one of the great engineering feats of the age.

Geologists bored holes into the seabed and shores to find out the hardness of the rock that the tunnel-boring machines would have to work through. Road and rail engineers calculated the optimum size for the tunnels and the layouts for the shuttle terminals. Biologists and conservationists predicted the environmental impact. Building engineers and contractors estimated the number of workers, digging and cutting machines, trucks and tunnel-wall materials needed. They, together with economists and bankers, worked out the likely cost of the project and how it would be funded privately. (Their estimate was $8,575 million, but this has been exceeded.)

▲ So that they could foresee some of the construction problems they would have to overcome, Eurotunnel engineers built this 105-feet-long model railroad system of the shuttle train terminals. They also made scale models of the tunnels and the road-and-rail connections.

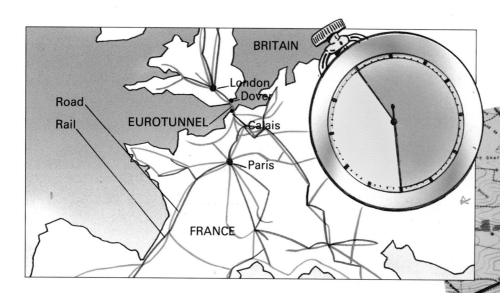

▲ In 1992, Europe becomes a single economic market. People and goods will be able to move freely to and from Britain and the Continent. Currently, London-to-Paris total passenger times are seven hours by ferry, five hours by hovercraft and three hours by airplane. With the opening of Eurotunnel, intercity rail journeys from center to center will be as fast as by airplane.

ALTERNATIVES REJECTED

The British and French governments accepted Eurotunnel in preference to three other plans. Euroroute consisted of artificial islands about five miles from the British and French coasts, with a road bridge and rail tunnel linking islands and shores. Channel Expressway was a combined road-and-rail tunnel bored through the seabed. Eurobridge comprised two giant towers and a suspended tube with four layers of traffic. Problems with the above-ground structures, such as bridges and islands, included whether they would stand up to heavy corrosion by saltwater, and resist the battering by strong winds and waves whipped up by the storms that sweep along the Channel.

▼ When choosing a site for the French terminal, engineers looked for flat land on which new railroad tracks could be laid easily, close to the Tunnel entrance. The best location was at Coquelles, south of Calais. The colored areas show how much land the terminals take up.

Artificial islands with a bridge for road traffic

A bored road tunnel with occasional trains

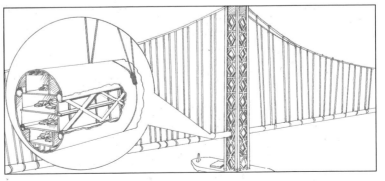

A bridge with suspended shell and four levels of traffic

WHICH ROUTE?

Geologists knew from previous attempts at building a Channel Tunnel, that the shortest undersea route would in fact not be the best. Beneath the Channel lie three main layers of rock: Middle Chalk, Lower Chalk, and Gault Clay. But only the lower part of the Lower Chalk is ideal for tunneling. The other layers consist of rock that is either too brittle and allows too much water to seep into the tunnel, or is too soft and weak to support the weight of the construction.

The route and depth of Eurotunnel was planned so that the maximum length would lie within favorable, "bore-friendly" rocks. The result is a winding path with gentle gradients at either end. The gradients will help both the acceleration and braking of trains and the draining of seawater that enters the Tunnel.

Most of the Tunnel's route is bored through chalk marl, which is a mixture of clay and chalk. On the French side, though, it will have to pass through layers of chalk that are cracked and leaky. A mixture of cement and clay will be injected into this rock ahead of the tunnel-boring machines, to strengthen it and make it watertight.

A winding route

At their closest points, the coasts of Britain and France are about 21 miles apart. Eurotunnel, to follow the best route through the seabed, will be 24 miles from coast to coast. On land there will be a total additional 7 miles of tunneling.

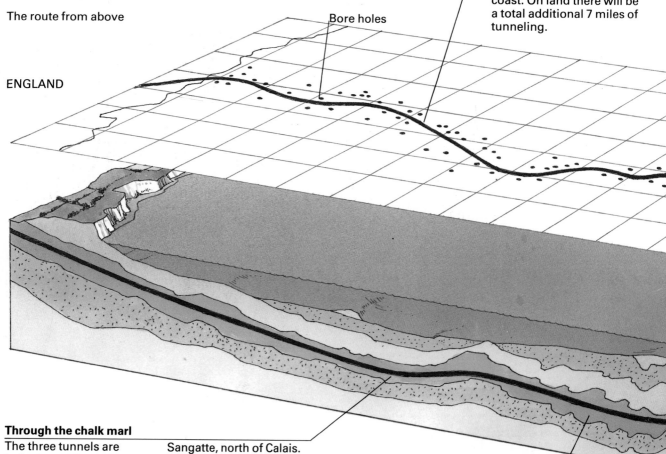

The route from above

Bore holes

ENGLAND

Through the chalk marl

The three tunnels are being bored through a gently curving layer of chalk from Castle Hill, north of Folkestone, to Beussingue Farm, near Sangatte, north of Calais. Only on the French side is tunneling having to be carried out through several different kinds of chalk layers.

Side view of the route

Geologists use three main survey methods: seismic studies, satellite mapping and boreholes. The first method involves ships dragging explosive devices through the water. Shock waves created by small blasts travel through the water and into the seabed rocks. The echoes from the different layers of chalk are detected at the surface. The direction and time delay of the echoes provide details of the rock structure. Satellite cameras provide photographs of the area. By boring down into the rock from offshore drill rigs, the depth and hardness of the rock layers are determined.

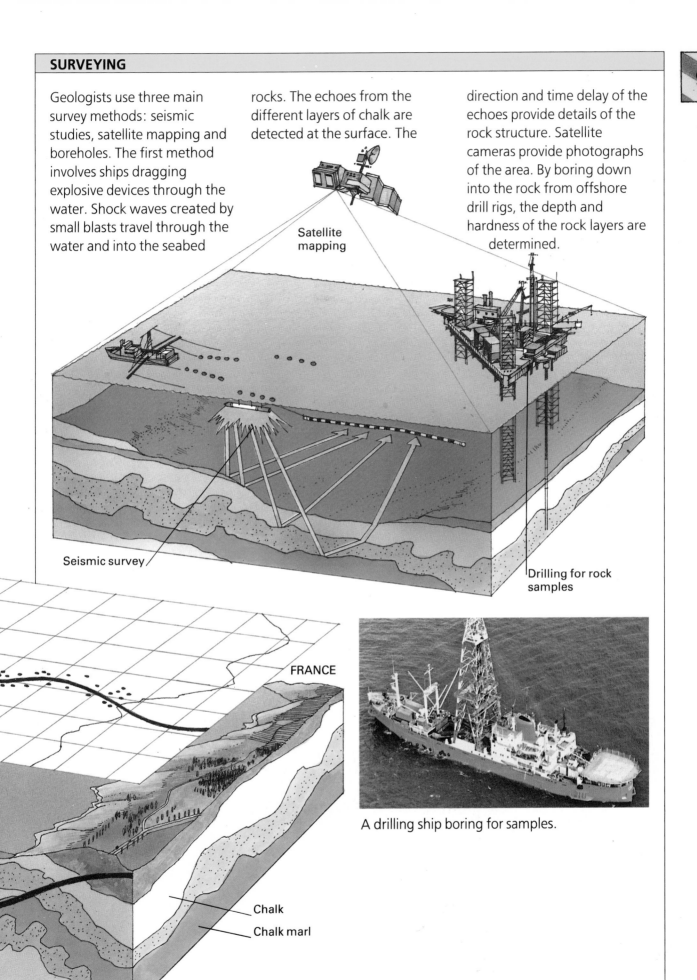

Satellite mapping

Seismic survey

Drilling for rock samples

FRANCE

Chalk

Chalk marl

A drilling ship boring for samples.

Three separate tunnels are being bored from both sides of the Channel. The red shaded areas show how far they had progressed by the end of 1989.

Access to the tunnels
At Shakespeare Cliff, tunneling is undertaken from a platform built behind a new seawall. When construction work is complete, the giant supply tunnels will be sealed off, but a few small passages will be left open for maintenance and repairs.

Tunneling to France
Now that the service tunnel has been bored, work on the two main tunnels has started. Tunnels are being bored at a rate of between about 2.6 and 5.58 feet per hour.

Entrance near Folkestone
The three tunnels will emerge at Castle Hill, five miles from the coastal construction site. The shuttle train terminal at Cheriton is being built close to the entrance.

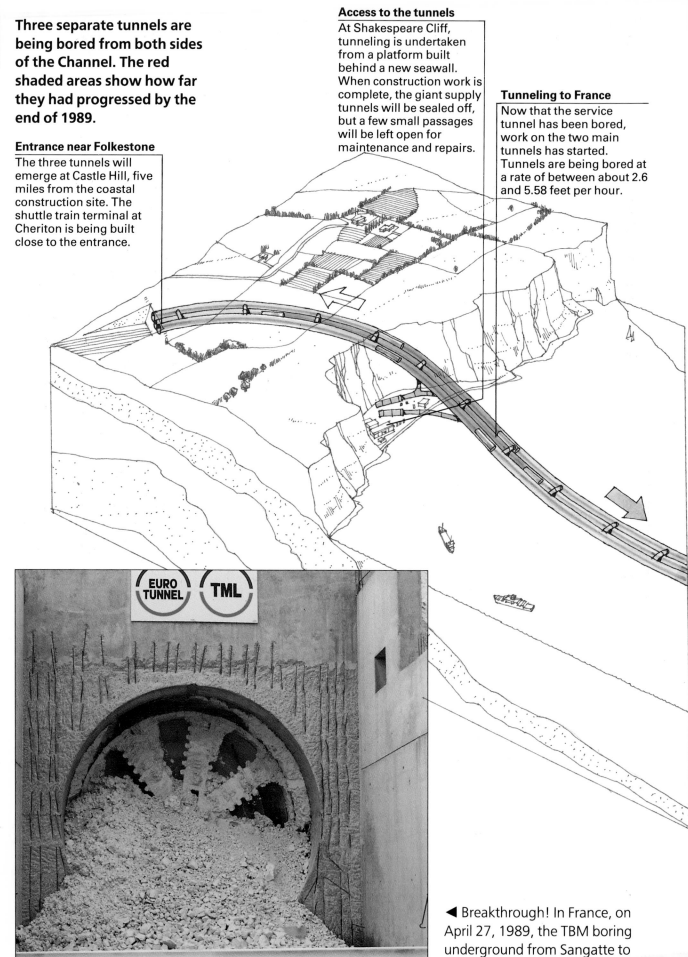

◀ Breakthrough! In France, on April 27, 1989, the TBM boring underground from Sangatte to Coquelles, finally emerged.

TUNNELING FOUR WAYS

Engineers have planned that Eurotunnel should be built from two construction sites and bored in four different directions. From a site at Shakespeare Cliff near Folkestone, tunneling is working outward toward France and inward toward the entrance at Castle Hill. On the French side, from Sangatte, tunneling is progressing through the seabed to a meeting point in mid-Channel, and also inland to Coquelles. The central service tunnel is being bored first, to act as a pilot, or test, tunnel.

As the tunnel-boring machines – TBMs – move forward, the ground ahead and to each side is examined. Wherever necessary, cracks in the chalk marl are filled with grout (a mixture of sand, cement and water) in preparation for the boring of the main tunnels. On both sides of the Channel, up to five TBMs are being used at the same time.

Tunneling to England

The French, drilling in the opposite direction through the seabed, are tunneling at a slower rate than the English, since they have to contend with more difficult and varied geological conditions. The British and French service tunnels are due to meet, mid-Channel, late in 1990.

French Tunnel entrance

The service tunnel from the construction site at Sangatte to the entrance at Coquelles has been successfully completed. Boring of the first of the main tunnels is now under way. The French land sections of the Tunnel are only 2 miles in length.

French construction site

At Sangatte, a giant shaft has been built in the shore. This houses a working platform from which the TBMs and the pumps that remove loose rock and earth (spoil) from the cutting face are operated.

BORING FROM ENGLAND

At Shakespeare Cliff the construction site is on two levels, the upper and lower. At the Upper Site, on top of the cliff, is an accommodation camp for the 400 or more tunnel workers, and access roads for construction traffic.

The lower site comprises a work platform beside the sea (see below), and the underground tunnel-boring and building area, shown here. All personnel and materials enter and leave the tunnel workings through four access tunnels. The supply tunnel leads from a store depot at the surface to the cross-Channel tunnels. Inside it are five special rail tracks along which electric locomotives pull supply cars from the surface, carrying down cables, concrete lining segments, and pipes. On their return journeys, they take spoil to the main conveyor, which carries it to the surface for disposal.

From this location, the TBMs are working outward in two directions: toward Castle Hill and to the mid-Channel meeting point. There is a constant movement of people, materials, spoil and machines.

TO TERMINAL

Supply tunnel

Main conveyor

To the surface
Waste soil and rock are brought to the surface by a long conveyor belt inside one of the sloping access tunnels.

▲ At the lower site, the work platform has been built on land created by constructing a new seawall and filling the space behind it with spoil from the tunnel workings.

Conveyors carrying the spoil.

Personnel access

A 33-feet diameter vertical access tunnel leads from the upper site to the underground workings. Tunnelers travel to and from their workplace in elevators, like those in a coal mine.

Elevators

Supply tunnel

From the main supply tunnel, branches of the special electric railway network cross-link and run into the three cross-Channel tunnels. As the TBMs work forward the rail tracks are extended, to carry materials and spoil to and from the workfaces.

STEEP SLOPES

The slope in the supply tunnel is so steep that ordinary locomotive wheels would constantly slip on the rails – going up as well as down. The locomotives have therefore been fitted with a rack-and-pinion (toothed-wheel and rail) system like the trains that run on steep mountainsides.

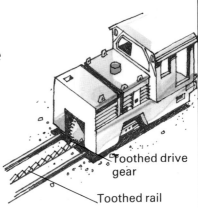

Toothed drive gear

Toothed rail

Loaded materials train

Rack locomotive

Spoil conveyor

Spoil conveyor

Spoil conveyor

Empty spoil cars

Conveying the spoil

Conveyor belts attached to the TBMs load spoil into empty cars. The cars transfer the spoil into bins, and from these it is carried to the surface by the main conveyor.

Spoil bin

Train dumping spoil

Spoil bin

TBM erection chamber

TO FRANCE

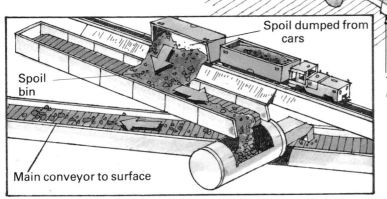

Spoil dumped from cars

Spoil bin

Main conveyor to surface

BORING FROM FRANCE

On the French side, a giant access shaft has been built in the shore. Within this the engineers have constructed dozens of tunnel-building and spoil-removal systems.

The shaft is more than 213 feet tall and 184 feet in diameter. Inside, 94 feet below ground level, is the main working platform. From here, the TBMs are working inland and out into the seabed, creating the cross-Channel tunnels. A system of conveyor belts and electric trains leads through the base of the shaft, removing spoil and bringing in construction materials.

At the top of the shaft are overhead cranes used to lower sections of tunnel lining onto the working platform and to help with the installation of the TBMs. Built along one side of the shaft are offices and changing rooms for the shaft workforce, which totals almost 1,800. The workers operate in shifts of 8 to 10 hours, and rarely come to the surface during that time. Within the shaft, food, drink and toilet facilities are all available. All activities in and around the shaft are monitored from a central control room that is filled with TV screens and computers.

Construction and operation of the Sangatte shaft is a remarkable feat of engineering. It is a self-contained building site with its own life-support system for the workforce and emergency services, comprising ambulance and fire-fighting equipment.

▼ To construct the shaft at Sangatte, first the outer perimeter wall was built. Then, using bulldozers, excavators and cranes, the earth inside was removed. Finally, the various platforms and supply systems were installed.

Grout
As soon as sections of tunnel lining are installed, the joints between them are filled with grout. This is made on site and pumped into a giant container in the shaft, through 1,115 feet of tubing.

Overhead cranes
There are two main crane systems. The largest, with a lifting capacity of 430 tons, is used to install the TBMs. The other system can carry loads of up to 60 tons. It is used to place tunnel linings in the shaft.

Manriders
Teams of 25 workers at a time travel from the changing rooms alongside the shaft to the worksite elevators in small trains, known as draisines or "manriders."

Batteries
Construction locomotives running in and out of the shaft to the TBMs are battery-powered so that diesel fumes do not fill the workplace. The batteries are regularly changed and recharged.

Elevators
There are a total of five elevators in the shaft: two ordinary, and three heavy-duty. The latter are fitted with train rails so that manriders can drive straight into them and exit directly into the railroad system at the base of the shaft.

Spoil from the face
Rock and earth are carried from the workfaces by trains to hoppers. These channel them onto conveyors leading to the crushers.

Dumped into crushers
Spoil is dumped into crushing machines beneath the working platform, where it is mixed with water and pumped out of the shaft.

Tunnel linings
Special flat-trailer cars are used to carry concrete and iron lining sections to the workfaces, where they are installed mechanically.

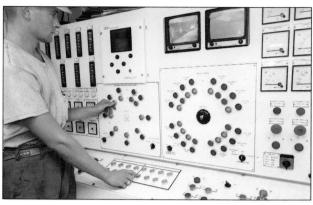

A French Tunnel-Boring Machine (TBM)

The Control room of a TBM

The cutting head

The rotating head is fitted with more than 100 cutting rollers and 200 picking "teeth." These are all made of tungsten, a very hard and tough metal also used for armor plating in tanks.

Hydraulic motor

This pushes forward or retracts the cutting teeth a few inches for maximum efficiency.

Steer shoes

Fine adjustment of the TBM's alignment is by means of a series of rams pushed against the walls.

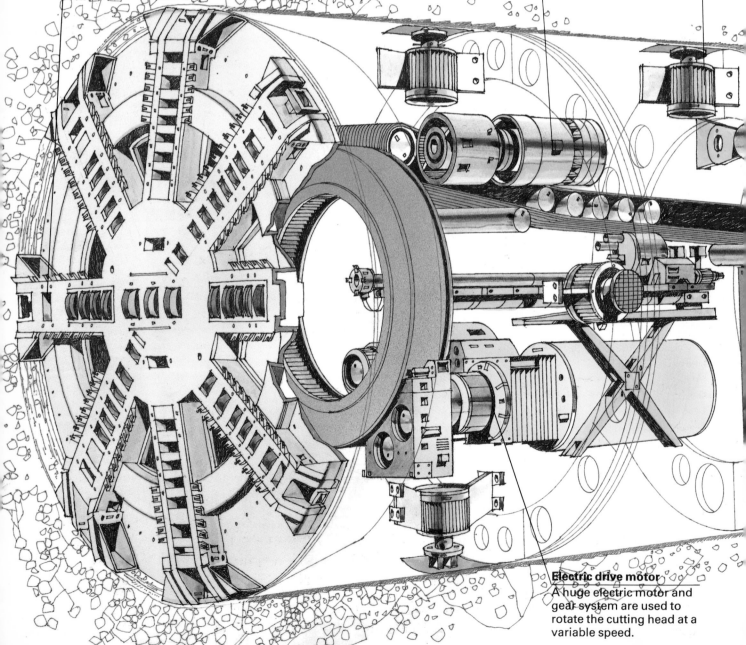

Electric drive motor

A huge electric motor and gear system are used to rotate the cutting head at a variable speed.

TBMs

Like a mole digging through soil, each TBM cuts its way through rock. The largest TBMs, used to build the main tunnels, each measure 29 feet in diameter, more than 49 feet in length and 1,300 tons in weight. Behind each TBM, in fact, there is a type of train – the construction train. More than 591 feet long and with over 1,000 tons of accessories, this contains a conveyor belt system for removing the spoil from the cutting face, and machinery for fitting concrete tunnel-lining segments to the cut out rock. It is constantly being moved forward to keep up with the TBM.

The gripper unit
The cutting head is fixed onto this section of the TBM, which is moved forward by means of four hydraulic rams and stabilized by gripper pads pushed firmly against the surrounding rock. The control cabin and start of the spoil conveyor are housed here, too.

Push rams
To bore forward, the cutting head must be pushed hard against the rock. This is the function of the hydraulic (fluid-pressure) push rams.

Conveyor

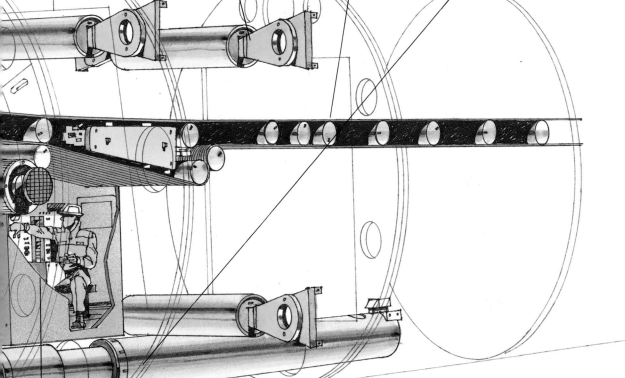

Computer control
The TBM operator sits in a control cabin equipped with closed-circuit television cameras, guidance system, and computerized monitoring equipment.

The TBMs and construction trains were built, a section at a time, at the Folkestone and Sangatte sites. Depending on the rock conditions, a TBM cutting head rotates 1.5 to 3 times each minute, and moves forward at about five inches in that time. For every five feet of progress, it cuts away 3,531 cubic feet of rock.

TUNNEL LININGS

As the TBMs work forward, segments of tunnel lining are fitted to the cut rock. The segments are brought to the workface on flat cars pushed by electric locomotives (see pages 12-13). The tunnel walls are made up of thousands of lining rings, each composed of several of the segments, each weighing between 3.5 and 8 tons.

On the English side, the lining segments are pushed together snugly, and the joints and the gaps between them and the surrounding rock filled with grout. On the French side, where it is necessary to make the lining more watertight, the segments are bolted together and fitted with rubber seals.

► Each ring of the tunnel is made up of at least six segments and is constructed in about 15 minutes. With 268 different shapes and sizes of segment, delivery of the correct segments to the right place, at the right time, is a complex task involving elaborate computer systems.

Lower segment erector
Segments forming the floor of each tunnel, on which a roadway or rail track is to be laid, are pushed down by rams.

Upper segment erector
Roof segments are taken from the conveyor belt and forced against the rockface with rams controlled by levers and gears.

Segment conveyor
An overhead crane lifts segments from the storage platform onto the conveyor belt. From here they pass to the erectors.

Altogether more than 700,000 concrete and iron lining segments will be used to build Eurotunnel. In England, the segments are being made at a factory on the Isle of Grain, east of London, and transported to Folkestone – nearly 28 miles away – by train. In France, they are made at Sangatte, at the same site as the access shaft, and are carried to the supply cars by mobile cranes. More than 600 people are involved in segment production and transportation.

Each concrete tunnel lining segment consists of a curved slab of concrete molded around a meshwork of metal rods and wire reinforcement. The concrete is hardened in giant heating rooms, a process that takes 6-8 hours. The segments are expected to last for at least 100 years before they are replaced.

Making tunnel lining segments

Positioning a tunnel lining segment

Spoil conveyor
This carries loose rock and earth from the TBM cutting head to waiting "muck cars" farther along the train.

Ventilation shaft
Giant ducts conduct fresh air into the work area and carry away vehicle and machinery fumes and spent air.

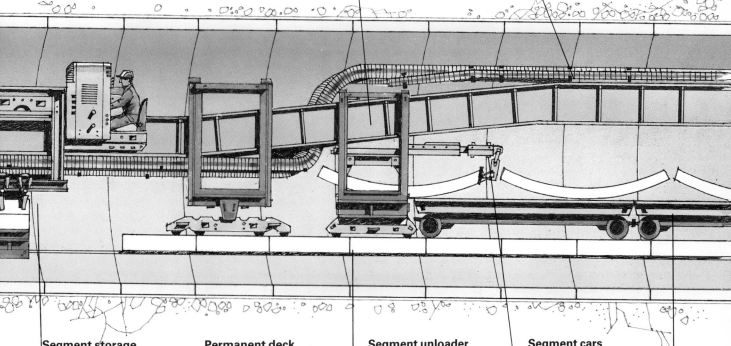

Segment storage
Segments are stacked on their side or flat, depending on their shape, size and construction. The rate of fitting the segments is matched by an equal rate of their delivery by the supply trains.

Permanent deck
Extending the full length of the construction train is a flat, solid floor along which all the mobile machinery moves. This, too, is made in sections of preformed concrete slabs.

Segment unloader
Lining and permanent deck segments are lifted from the cars by crane, one at a time.

Segment cars
About six cars at a time are used to carry concrete and iron segments to the workface. This is sufficient for two complete rings of the tunnel and the corresponding extension of the permanent deck.

THE TAIL END

There is just as much activity going on at the rear of each TBM construction train, as there is at the front! About every half-hour a pair of locomotives passes through, hauling 20 or more cars at a time. This train runs on rails fitted to the permanent deck. There are two types of car: flatbeds for carrying tunnel-building materials, and open cars for trains transporting rubble and earth from the cutting head. Each spoil car can carry about 494 cubic feet – enough to fill an average-sized room of a normal house.

At the end of each work shift, a riding car attached to the front locomotive carries a new team of tunnelers to the site and takes away the tired team. Throughout the day, the spoil conveyor belt brings muck from the TBM and drops it into the waiting empty cars. And as tunnel-boring progresses, machinery and equipment are extended or dismantled and moved along, in order to keep pace with the cutting head. These include cranes, erectors, loaders, mechanical arms and hydraulic rams, as well as lighting, ventilation and communications systems.

Throughout the tail end of the construction train – the rear 131 feet shown here – the tunnel lining has been completed and fully grouted and sealed.

Moving conveyor
The spoil conveyor belt is more than 328 feet in length and can carry hundreds of cubic feet of muck in one hour.

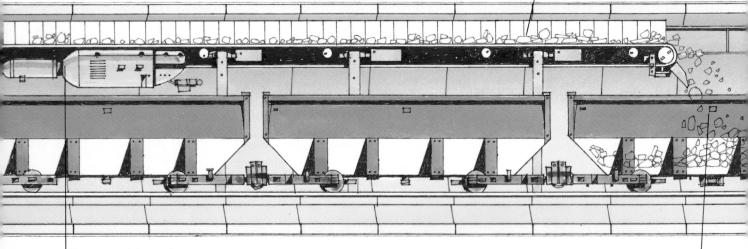

Conveyor drive unit
An electric motor and gear system keeps the spoil conveyor belt in constant motion.

Loading spoil
One after the other, empty cars are moved into position beneath the end of the spoil conveyor.

KEEPING STRAIGHT

Laser beams are used to check that the TBMs follow a straight line through the rock. These light beams are rodlike and spread out very little, even over several miles. They are also used like plumblines, spirit levels, and rulers, to check that construction train machinery is exactly vertical or horizontal. By lining up a number of laser beams, engineers can measure small changes in position, or movements of equipment.

▲ Equipment and tunnelers are brought to the tail end by train cars which also take back the spoil.

Support systems
The tail end is filled with electric cables for lighting and machinery, and ventilation ducts.

Extending ventilation
From a moving platform, new sections of ventilation duct are added as the construction train moves forward.

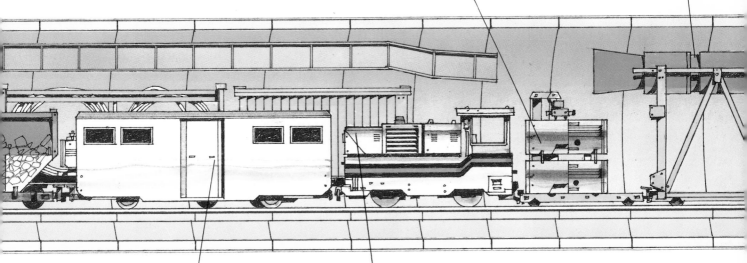

Riding car
Up to 25 tunnelers at a time are transported in a special personnel car, to and from the worksite.

Locomotive
The electric locos are only about 20 feet long and 7 feet high, but they can pull more than 200 tons.

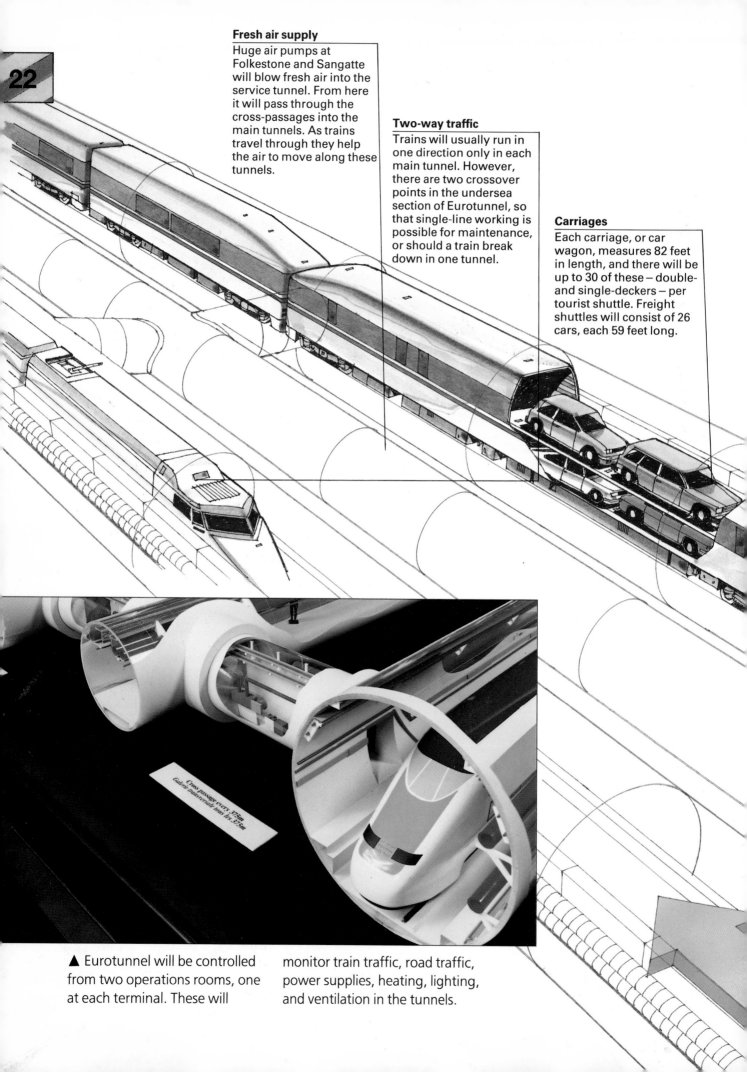

Fresh air supply
Huge air pumps at Folkestone and Sangatte will blow fresh air into the service tunnel. From here it will pass through the cross-passages into the main tunnels. As trains travel through they help the air to move along these tunnels.

Two-way traffic
Trains will usually run in one direction only in each main tunnel. However, there are two crossover points in the undersea section of Eurotunnel, so that single-line working is possible for maintenance, or should a train break down in one tunnel.

Carriages
Each carriage, or car wagon, measures 82 feet in length, and there will be up to 30 of these – double- and single-deckers – per tourist shuttle. Freight shuttles will consist of 26 cars, each 59 feet long.

▲ Eurotunnel will be controlled from two operations rooms, one at each terminal. These will monitor train traffic, road traffic, power supplies, heating, lighting, and ventilation in the tunnels.

At all times, conditions within Eurotunnel will be suitable not only for the safe and comfortable transit of train passengers, but also to allow routine inspection and maintenance of the structure and its equipment. An efficient ventilation system will ensure that there is no buildup of fumes from machinery.

Locomotives

The electric 99 mph shuttle locomotives will run on the same size (gauge) track as the through trains, but their greater body width and height mean they will not be able to travel on the ordinary European rail networks.

Four different types of train will run through Eurotunnel, providing rapid, reliable, round-the-clock transportation between Britain and the Continent. At peak times, up to 18 trains each hour will be whistling through in each direction. Most frequent will be the tourist shuttles. These will travel between the terminals at Cheriton and Coquelles and take automobiles, campers, buses, motorcycles, bicycles, and their passengers. The journey time will be about 35 minutes. Running less often, and more slowly, will be freight shuttles transporting trucks.

High-speed passenger trains and overnight sleeper trains – up to four each hour – will travel through the Tunnel, on their way between London's proposed new international rail terminal at Waterloo, and major European cities such as Paris, Brussels and Frankfurt. Finally the container-car, transporter, and bulk-load trains will carry freight between all parts of Britain and mainland Europe. By using Eurotunnel, it will be possible to deliver several boxes of this book from a printer in England to a shop in Holland, on the same day.

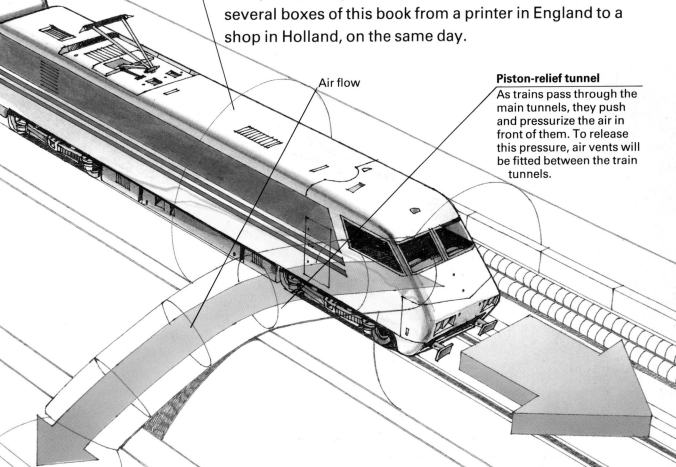

Air flow

Piston-relief tunnel

As trains pass through the main tunnels, they push and pressurize the air in front of them. To release this pressure, air vents will be fitted between the train tunnels.

THE TERMINALS

At both Cheriton and Coquelles terminals, engineers have planned four main areas: toll booths where tickets are purchased; passport and customs control; stores and refreshments; and vehicle loading and unloading platforms. When complete, the English site will cover more than 350 acres and the French site 1,750 acres. (A soccer pitch is about two and a half acres.)

The terminals are already two of the largest construction sites in Europe. Bridges, access roads, flyovers, railway tracks and platforms are all being built, often using new methods of engineering. Some bridges, for instance, instead of first being fully designed and then constructed, are being planned and built in stages.

Loading the top deck

From a high platform, automobiles will drive onto the upper deck of double-decker cars. A special ramp will bridge the gap between platform and car.

▲ Full-sized models of the shuttle cars have been made, to ensure that loading and unloading will be rapid and safe.

Shuttle trains will be made up of several carrier cars and a locomotive at each end. At the rear will be one or more special loading cars, and at the front one or more for unloading. On departure, automobiles and trucks enter the shuttle and drive straight down inside the cars or sections until they are all full. Then the loading doors shut and the train moves off. At the other end, the vehicles drive off in procession.

Having completed frontier checks, vehicles will drive across bridges over the tracks to the platforms, for loading. On arrival at the destination terminal, they will be able to join the roadway network without further checks. (The Single European Trade Market of 1992 may see an end to duty-free shopping and checks.)

▲ A scale model of the terminal in England shows the complex arrangement of rail lines and platforms.

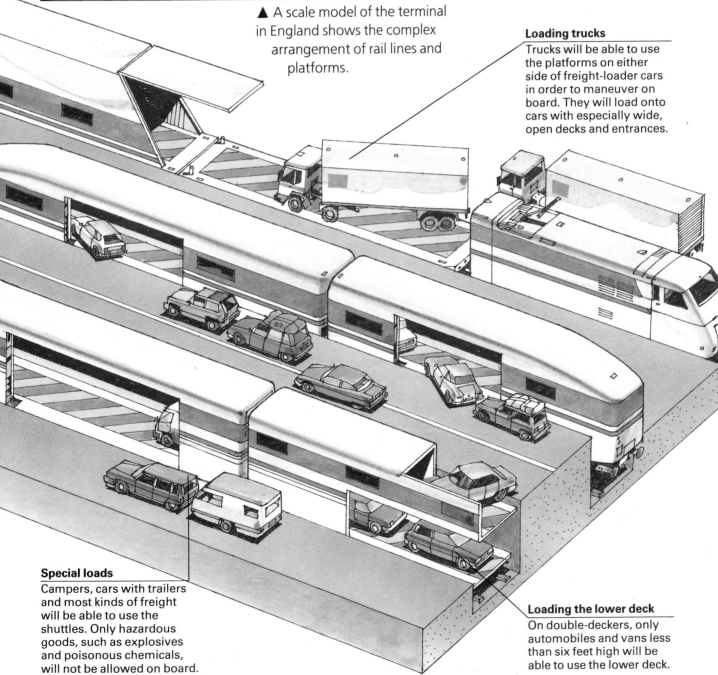

Loading trucks
Trucks will be able to use the platforms on either side of freight-loader cars in order to maneuver on board. They will load onto cars with especially wide, open decks and entrances.

Special loads
Campers, cars with trailers and most kinds of freight will be able to use the shuttles. Only hazardous goods, such as explosives and poisonous chemicals, will not be allowed on board.

Loading the lower deck
On double-deckers, only automobiles and vans less than six feet high will be able to use the lower deck.

SAFETY FIRST

Eurotunnel incorporates a wide range of safety features. These should ensure that in the event of a rail accident, breakdown, or fire, emergency services will be on the scene in minutes, and passengers will reach the open air quickly and with a minimum of risk. There will also be systems to prevent the tunnels being flooded, and to stop wild animals infected with rabies passing through from France to Britain.

Most of the safety features will be located in the service tunnel and its passageways. In the main tunnels there will be a range of surveillance and monitoring equipment. In the case of an emergency, passengers should leave a train and enter the service tunnel. From here they will walk or be taken by bus, or by train in the other main tunnel, to the exit. It is estimated that all passengers – up to 1,500 per train – could be evacuated from the Tunnel well within 90 minutes.

Eurotunnel will operate using a number of "backup" and "fail-safe" systems. Should one control center shut down, the other automatically takes over. If the power supply from either terminal fails, the other terminal will switch electricity to both halves of the Tunnel. Trains then still run, but more slowly and less often.

Fire fighting vehicle
In the event of a fire, fire tenders drive along the roadway in the service tunnel to the cross-passageways. Fire hoses will be connected to a tunnel water-pipe system supplied with fresh water from each shore. Fire fighters will also use portable extinguishers.

Emergency telephone

Air dampers
Doors leading from the main tunnels into the service tunnel are to be fitted with grilles that allow air to pass through in only one direction. This prevents the "piston effect" on air of passing trains reaching the service tunnel.

Airflow
Air pressure in the service tunnel will be kept at a higher level than in the main tunnels. This aims to ensure good ventilation of the trains and carriages.

Emergency transportation
Police, ambulance, and fire crews rush to the scene of an accident in special vehicles from each terminal. The emergency crews will be trained to operate Eurotunnel's special safety equipment.

CHANGING TRACKS

There are two train crossover points, roughly one-third of the distance into Eurotunnel, under the sea at each end. Should a train break down in the tunnel, passengers will transfer via the service tunnel to the other train. Trains will then run in both directions along one track.

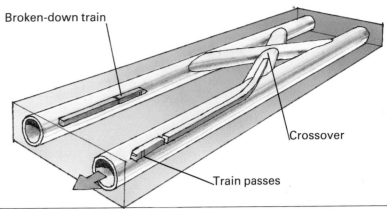

Broken-down train

Crossover

Train passes

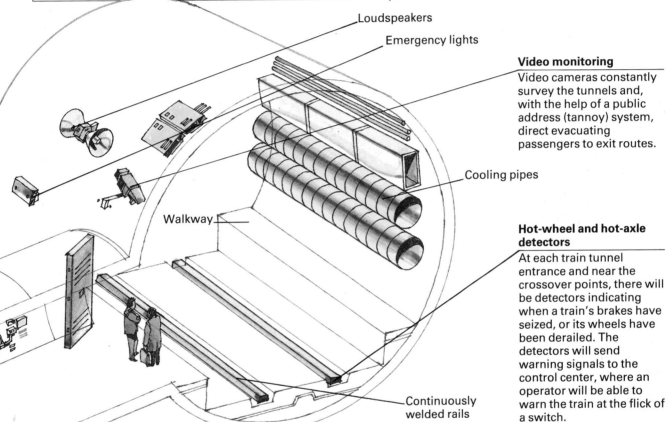

Loudspeakers

Emergency lights

Video monitoring

Video cameras constantly survey the tunnels and, with the help of a public address (tannoy) system, direct evacuating passengers to exit routes.

Cooling pipes

Hot-wheel and hot-axle detectors

At each train tunnel entrance and near the crossover points, there will be detectors indicating when a train's brakes have seized, or its wheels have been derailed. The detectors will send warning signals to the control center, where an operator will be able to warn the train at the flick of a switch.

Walkway

Continuously welded rails

▶ Passengers stay in their cars during the shuttle journey. Should a fire break out in a shuttle car, automatic fire extinguishers switch on and fire doors seal the car from the rest of the train. Fire crews should be on the scene in minutes.

THE YOUNG ENGINEER

Modern tunneling dates back to the start of the Industrial Revolution in Europe, in the 1700s. Then, tunnels were built to take canals underground. The principles of construction developed by the 18th-century engineers are the same as those now being used to build the Channel Tunnel. Try the projects shown here, which demonstrate some of the basic scientific laws involved in designing and constructing a tunnel. All of these principles are being used in Eurotunnel on a much larger scale! Look back through the book and find where they appear.

Tunnel shapes

Tunnel walls are curved or arched to give greatest strength (page 18). Place a curved sheet of cardboard between two bricks and put bricks on top of the cardboard, one at a time. The weight of the load is evenly distributed and shared between the two curved sides. Now lay a flat sheet of cardboard between two bricks. Again, add bricks one at a time. This time, the load is concentrated in the middle of the cardboard. Compare the strength of the curved and flat "tunnel walls" by adding bricks until each collapses under the strain. Which is strongest? How does a V-shaped wall stand up to loads?

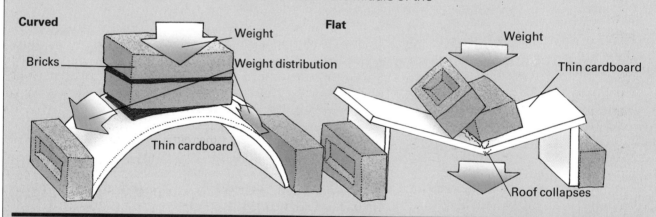

Curved

Weight

Bricks

Weight distribution

Thin cardboard

Flat

Weight

Thin cardboard

Roof collapses

Piston-relief tunnels

As trains move fast through a tunnel, they compress the air in front of them (page 23). To prevent a buildup of air pressure, Eurotunnel has a number of piston-relief tunnels. You can see for yourself how these will allow high-pressure air to escape. Compare the force of air on a feather when you blow – first through a straw with holes cut in it, and second through one without holes. How does the diameter of the straw affect the air flow? Try blowing with wider or narrower straws.

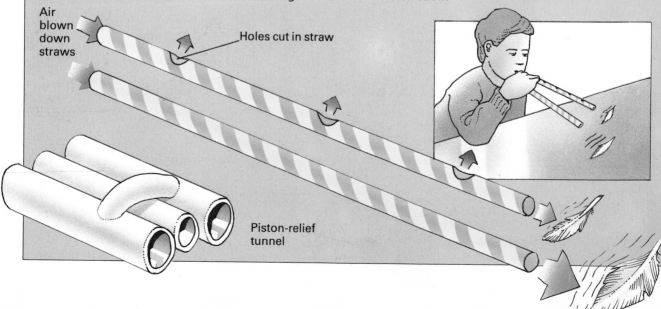

Air blown down straws

Holes cut in straw

Piston-relief tunnel

Drilling holes

There are two ways of boring tunnels. Tunnels in rock are generally made by drilling and blasting with dynamite. Those in soft ground are bored by scraping – and then immediately supporting the walls with lining segments. However Eurotunnel, being built through the seabed, is not being bored using explosives, for fear of water pouring in. And it is too large to drill or scrape out using ordinary tunneling machines. The rotating cutting heads of the TBMs are fitted with hundreds of cutting rollers and teeth that pick and scrape away at the rock. You can see how effective this is. First, compare the effort needed to chisel and electrically drill a hole in solid wood. Then, using the base of a plastic bottle as shown opposite, see how you can bore a tunnel in wet sand.

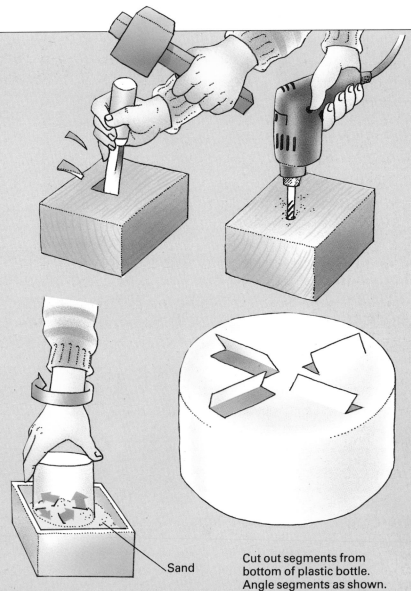

Sand

Cut out segments from bottom of plastic bottle. Angle segments as shown.

Hydraulic pistons

The TBM cutting head is pushed hard against the rockface using pistons like those in a bicycle pump. Unlike a bicycle pump, though, which is filled with air, the TBM pistons are filled with liquid. But the effect is the same, as you can try for yourself. Put a paper bag under a pile of books. Then blow air into the bag. Because fluids are hard to compress, they can be used to transfer pressure from, say, your lungs to the books – or from a piston ram to the TBM cutting head!

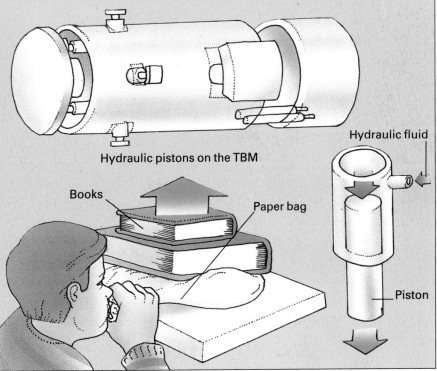

Hydraulic pistons on the TBM

Books

Paper bag

Hydraulic fluid

Piston

TUNNELS WORLDWIDE

Tunnels are being used increasingly in road and rail transportation, for several reasons. They can follow the most direct route between two places. They can be used in any weather conditions. They can be built without disrupting existing communications. And they do not disturb the scenery or environment too much.

Tunnels are some of the biggest structures that engineers have ever built. Some that run under water, like the Chesapeake Bay Tunnel in America are built by sinking giant tubes onto the seabed. The tubes are floated into position, their sides are filled with concrete, and then they are lowered into a pre-dug trench. The tubes are joined together and the water is pumped out. Tunnels that take vehicle-carrying trains, like Eurotunnel, already exist in many regions. One example is the Simplon Tunnel, which is not under the seabed – but through the Alps linking Switzerland and Italy.

NAME	COUNTRY (REGION)	LENGTH	TYPE
West Delaware	United States (New York City)	105 mi	Water supply
Seikan	Japan (Honshu to Hokkaido)	33 mi	Undersea rail
Oshimizu	Japan (near Tokyo)	14 mi	Rail
Simplon	Switzerland-Italy	12 mi	Rail
Moscow Metro	USSR	19 mi	Metro railway
St Gottard	Switzerland (Goschenen-Airolo)	10 mi	Road
Orange-Fish Rivers	South Africa	51 mi	Irrigation
Chesapeake Bay	United States (Virginia)	18 mi	Road bridges and tunnel
Rove	France (Marseilles to Rhone)	45 mi	Canal
Majes	Peru	61 mi	Hydroelectricity
When completed in 1993			
Eurotunnel	Britain-France	31 mi	Undersea rail

Mt Blanc road tunnel through the Alps

Seikan – the longest rail tunnel in the world

GLOSSARY

Access shaft Tunnel or passageway through which people can enter a site.

Concrete A mixture of cement, fine aggregate (sand), coarse aggregate (gravel or small stones) and water, that sets hard. The setting is a chemical reaction, not a drying-out, so it takes place even under water.

Conveyor An endless moving belt that carries objects from one place to another.

Cutting head The boring tool of a Tunnel Boring Machine (TBM). It scrapes, picks, and grinds away at the rockface.

Deck A floor or platform suspended from a bridge or built across the base of a ship, tunnel or similar construction.

Foundations The base of a building, that transmits its weight safely into the surrounding subsoil and rock and stops it sinking or leaning.

Geology The science of the nature of soils and rocks and, in engineering, how these affect the construction and stability of buildings.

Grout A mixture of cement, water, and fine sand that sets hard and is waterproof when dry. It is used to fill cracks and joints in concrete segments.

Hydraulic Worked by fluid under pressure.

Ram A machine that repeatedly drops or pushes a heavy weight onto or into something, or that uses pressure to force something to move forward.

Reinforced concrete Concrete that sets around metal rods, girders, or meshes, to give it greater strength.

Services Electricity, water, drainage, gas, and other supplies.

Shuttle A regular back-and-forth service between two terminals (rail, sea, air, etc.)

Spoil Loose rock, earth, sand, and mud, removed from an excavation or tunnel-boring site.

Steel Iron from a blast furnace that has had nearly all the carbon removed (down to 1.7 percent or less) and small quantities of other substances added. There are many types of steel, made hard and tough for various specialized applications.

Surveying The accurate measuring and plotting on a map of the geographical and geological features of a location.

Terminal A main arrival and departure point for train, sea, or air passengers.

Through-services Transportation system that operates on the same routes as shuttle services, but does not operate between the terminals.

Ventilation Some combination of warming, cooling, drying and moistening (humidifying) the air in a building or structure, to make it pleasant for people and suitable for delicate machinery.

INDEX

Photographic Credits:
Cover and all pages to page 30: Q.A. Photos Ltd; page 30 left: Rex Features; page 30 right: Spectrum Colour Library.

PRINTED IN BELGIUM BY
proost
INTERNATIONAL BOOK PRODUCTION